LAURELS OF LIFE

A Free-Verse Poetry Collection

Copyright Page

Cover design by S S Dhar
Product Form: Paperback
ISBN: 978-93-5692-808-4

Published/Authored by S S Dhar.

Dedication

For those who kept going
without applause,
without certainty,
without guarantees—
and still showed up.

Author's Note

This book does not promise answers.

It offers moments—
some quiet, some heavy, some unfinished—
the way life often gives them.

These poems were written to sit beside you,
not ahead of you.
To name what many feel
but rarely say out loud.

If you recognize yourself in these pages,
then the book has done its work.

Table of Contents

SECTION I — Beginnings & Becoming

First Light

I don't remember
my first breath,
but I remember the feeling
of arriving—

the quiet shock
of being here,
the way life begins
without asking
what kind of world
it is about to enter.

What We Are Given

Some of us inherit warmth.
Some inherit silence.

Some grow up learning
how to speak.
Others grow up learning
when not to.

The House That Raised Me

The house I grew up in
was not large,
but it held many moods.

Mornings smelled like routine—
tea cooling on tables,
shoes placed carefully by the door,
the quiet urgency of adults
already tired.

The walls heard everything.
Arguments whispered late at night.
Laughter that tried to stay light.
Dreams discussed softly,
as if speaking them too loudly
might make them disappear.

I learned early
that a home is not just shelter.
It is a teacher.

It teaches you how to listen.
How to wait.
How to become small
or brave
depending on the day.

Long after I left,
I carried it with me—
not the rooms,
but the lessons hiding inside them.

Schoolyard Economics

We learned math in classrooms
and worth on playgrounds.

Who had better shoes.
Who spoke without fear.
Who learned early
how to disappear
into the background.

Names

A name is the first thing
we are given
and the first thing
we spend years
learning how to live up to.

The Quiet Child

I was not loud.
I was observant.

While others rushed toward attention,
I learned how to watch—
how stories unfold,
how moods change,
how people reveal themselves
when they think no one is looking.

Teachers called it shyness.
Relatives called it politeness.

But it was something else.

It was the beginning
of learning the world
before deciding
how to speak to it.

Lessons Without Words

Some lessons arrive
without explanation—

the look on a parent's face,
the silence after a question,
the moment you realize
not everything is safe to ask.

Becoming Aware

There is a moment
when childhood loosens its grip.

You notice
how adults carry worry
like a second spine.
How money enters conversations
before dreams do.
How kindness is sometimes strategic.

It isn't betrayal.
It's awakening.

You don't lose innocence—
you outgrow it.

And in that space,
between wonder and awareness,
you begin assembling
the person
you will spend your life becoming.

Early Failures

Failure came quietly—
a missed chance,
a wrong answer,
a door that didn't open.

No speeches.
No explanations.
Just the feeling
of standing still
while others moved forward.

What I Learned From Watching

I learned more
from what wasn't said
than from what was.

I watched people stay
in places that shrank them.
I watched others leave
without knowing where they were going.

I learned that courage
often looks like patience.
That fear sometimes wears
the mask of responsibility.

Most of all,
I learned that everyone is guessing—
some just hide it better than others.

The First Want

Before ambition,
before plans,
before language—

there was want.
A quiet pull toward something unnamed.
A sense that life
held more
than what was visible.

Growing Questions

Why do some people get chances
and others get instructions?

Why does effort
not always equal reward?

Why does becoming older
feel less like gaining answers
and more like choosing
which questions
to live with?

The Edge of Becoming

Standing on the edge of youth,
I felt both eager and unprepared.

I wanted meaning
without knowing its cost.
Freedom without understanding its weight.

No one explained
that becoming yourself
is not a single moment,
but a long negotiation
between who you are
and who life keeps asking you to be.

Before the Fall

There was a moment—
brief, almost invisible—
before struggle became real.

Before life tested
what I believed about myself.

I didn't know then
how much I would need
the person
I was still becoming.

SECTION II — Pain, Loss & Survival

The First Real Loss

Loss does not announce itself.
It arrives like a change in weather—
sudden, undeniable,
and indifferent
to whether you were ready.

What Broke Quietly

Some things don't shatter.
They thin.

Trust thins.
Hope thins.
The belief that effort alone
will protect you.

You keep functioning—
showing up, replying, nodding—
while something essential
slips out of reach.

No one notices
because you haven't fallen apart.

That's the danger of quiet damage:
it convinces the world
you are fine
while teaching you
how to carry weight
without asking for help.

Long Season of Trying

There was a stretch of time
where effort felt invisible.

I worked, adjusted, learned, failed,
then worked again—
not dramatically,
not heroically,
just persistently.

Days blurred into each other.
Weeks passed without evidence
that anything was changing.

I began questioning the math of life.
If time plus effort
did not equal progress,
what was I missing?

People offered advice
from places of comfort.
"Be patient."
"Everything happens for a reason."

But patience feels different
when rent is due,
when self-doubt speaks louder than faith,
when sleep becomes a negotiation
between worry and exhaustion.

Still, I stayed.

Not because I was brave,
but because leaving
felt like erasing myself entirely.

Survival, I learned,
is sometimes choosing
the slow path forward
over the sudden relief of quitting.

Rejection Letters

Some no's arrive politely.
Others arrive silently.

Both teach the same lesson:
the world does not owe you
recognition for trying.

When Strength Is Expected

People admire resilience
without asking
what it costs.

They praise consistency
without noticing
how often you wanted to stop.

Strength becomes an expectation—
not a choice.

And somewhere along the way,
you forget
that it was once
something you had to build
from nothing.

The Night I Didn’t Call Anyone

There are nights
you don’t reach out.

Not because no one exists,
but because you’re tired
of explaining.

You rehearse the conversation in your head—
the concern,
the advice,
the well-meaning comparisons—
and decide silence
is simpler.

That night,
I sat with my thoughts
like they were unfinished sentences.

I questioned my decisions.
I replayed moments
where things might have gone differently.
I wondered how many lives exist
inside the life we end up living.

No breakdown.
No tears that demanded attention.

Just the steady weight
of being awake
when the world is asleep.

Loneliness isn't always about absence.
Sometimes it's about carrying
too much
without knowing
where to set it down.

Survival Mode

There is a version of you
that does not dream.

It only manages.
It only endures.
It keeps the lights on
and the questions quiet.

What Pain Teaches Slowly

Pain is not a lesson.
It's a process.

It strips away assumptions.
It rearranges priorities.
It shows you
how little control
you ever had.

And if you stay long enough,
it teaches you
how to stand
without applause,
how to move forward
without certainty.

Grief Without Ceremony

Some griefs
don't receive sympathy cards.

They exist quietly—
lost opportunities,
unspoken goodbyes,
versions of life
that never arrived.

The Weight of Continuing

Continuing is heavier
than quitting.

Quitting offers clarity.
Continuing demands faith
without evidence.

Every day you choose to stay,
you carry yesterday's doubt
into today's effort.

And still—
you wake up.
You try again.

That counts more
than anyone ever says.

The Shape of Endurance

Endurance does not look heroic.

It looks like alarms set early.
Meals eaten without appetite.
Dreams postponed but not buried.

It looks like choosing responsibility
over escape,
routine over relief.

I learned that endurance
is not about how much you can take,
but how gently
you learn to carry yourself
through the taking.

Some days,
the only victory
is that you did not become bitter.

That you stayed open
in a world that kept closing doors.

That you trusted—
not blindly,
but deliberately—
that survival
was shaping something useful
inside you.

Still Standing

I didn't win.
I didn't lose.

I remained.

Before the Shift

There comes a moment—
quiet, unannounced—
when pain stops being
the main character.

And something else
asks for attention.

Learning to Breathe Again

Recovery isn't dramatic.
It's subtle.

It's laughter that surprises you.
Sleep that comes without negotiation.
The return of curiosity.

You don't forget the past—
you integrate it.

And slowly,
you remember
that survival
was never the destination.

What Survived

After everything,
something remained—

not innocence,
not certainty,
but the willingness
to keep becoming.

SECTION III — Work, Dreams & Identity

Learning the Language of Effort

No one teaches you
how much of life
is repetition.

How many mornings
look identical
before anything changes.

The Resume Version of Me

On paper,
I am efficient.

I list achievements
without mentioning exhaustion.
I summarize years
into bullet points.

There is no space
for hesitation,
for doubt,
for the nights spent wondering
if I chose correctly.

The resume does not show
how many times I almost quit,
or how often confidence arrived
after the work was already done.

Still, I send it out—
not because it tells the whole truth,
but because it opens doors
that honesty alone
cannot.

The Cost of Wanting More

Wanting more
is rarely about greed.

It's about rest without fear.
Choice without consequence.
Dignity without explanation.

I watched people confuse ambition
with arrogance,
as if striving
were a moral failure.

But ambition,
when honest,
is simply the refusal
to remain unfinished.

There were years
where wanting more
made me lonely.
Where stability demanded silence,
and growth required risk.

I balanced responsibility
like fragile glass—
one wrong move
and everything could shatter.

Still, the want remained.

Not loud.
Not impatient.
Just steady.

A reminder
that comfort and fulfillment
are not always the same place.

Money Conversations

Money enters quietly,
then speaks loudly.

It decides who rests,
who worries,
who gets time to dream.

Burnout Isn't Laziness

Burnout doesn't announce itself.
It disguises itself as discipline.

You keep going
long after the joy leaves.
You confuse persistence
with progress.

Rest feels undeserved.
Stopping feels dangerous.

By the time you notice,
you are functioning
without feeling.

That's when you learn:
ambition without care
eventually consumes itself.

The Middle Years

Not young enough
to believe anything is possible.
Not old enough
to stop trying.

This is where most lives
actually happen.

Building a Name

A name is not built
through announcements.

It's built quietly—
through consistency,
through showing up
when it's inconvenient.

Recognition arrives late,
if at all.

And by then,
you've already learned
whether the work itself
was worth doing.

Identity Crisis, Adult Edition

At some point,
you stop asking
who you want to be—

and start asking
who you can live with becoming.

The Long Way Forward

Progress is uneven.

Some years sprint.
Some years stall.
Some years undo
what you thought was settled.

I stopped expecting linear growth
once I understood
how much of life
is corrective.

You try.
You misjudge.
You adjust.

There is no applause
for recalibration,
no ceremony
for choosing better
after choosing wrong.

Still, the long way forward
teaches patience
that shortcuts never could.

It teaches humility—
not as self-doubt,
but as accuracy.

Knowing where you stand
without exaggeration.

Knowing when to push
and when to wait.

This is not failure.
It is fluency
in the language of living.

Work as Mirror

Your work reflects
what you tolerate,
what you prioritize,
what you believe
you deserve.

Success, Redefined

Success changed shape
once I stopped chasing approval.

It became quieter.
More personal.

Enough income to breathe.
Enough time to think.
Enough peace
to sleep without rehearsing tomorrow.

No trophies.
No speeches.

Just alignment—
between effort and meaning.

When Comparison Creeps In

Comparison waits patiently.

It enters when you're tired,
when scrolling replaces rest,
when someone else's highlight
looks like your behind-the-scenes.

Staying Honest With Myself

There are easier paths.
There are louder paths.

I chose the honest one—
not because it's noble,
but because pretending
is exhausting.

I learned that integrity
is not perfection,
but consistency
between values and action.

The Last Long Night at Work

That night,
the building was quiet.

Lights hummed.
Screens glowed.
Everyone else had gone home.

I looked at my reflection
in the dark glass
and wondered
how many versions of me
had led to this moment.

I wasn't unhappy.
I wasn't fulfilled.

I was somewhere in between—
where most effort actually lives.

I realized then
that identity isn't discovered.

It's assembled—
decision by decision,
boundary by boundary,
day by ordinary day.

That understanding
didn't change everything.

But it changed enough.

Still Wanting

Even now,
after progress,
after proof—

the wanting remains.

Not hunger.
Not greed.

Just motion.

SECTION IV — Love, Time & Human Bonds

Love, Early Draft

At first,
love felt urgent.

Later,
it learned how to wait.

The People Who Stayed

Not everyone leaves.

Some people remain quietly—
through changes,
through seasons
where you are less impressive.

They don't demand explanations.
They don't rush your becoming.

They learn your silences.
They understand your pauses.

Over time,
their presence stops feeling special
and starts feeling essential.

That's how you know
it's real.

Distance

Distance doesn't always mean absence.

Sometimes it's just
two lives growing
in different directions
without resentment.

Loving Imperfectly

I stopped expecting love
to be seamless.

I stopped believing
that care arrives
without misunderstanding.

Real love hesitates.
It missteps.
It apologizes.

It stays curious
when certainty would be easier.

Conversations With My Parents

As they aged,
their advice softened.

Not wiser—
just gentler.

Time Between Friends

Friendships change
without permission.

Jobs, families, geography—
life edits the closeness.

Still,
some connections survive
on shared memory alone.

A laugh remembered.
A version of yourself
that existed only with them.

The Love That Didn't Last

Not every ending
is a failure.

Some love exists
only long enough
to teach you something
about yourself.

Aging

Aging isn't about wrinkles.

It's about realizing
how fast
ordinary days disappear.

What Forgiveness Actually Is

Forgiveness isn't approval.

It's release.

It's deciding
not to carry
what already took enough.

You don't forget.
You don't rewrite history.

You just stop letting it
define your posture
toward the future.

Shared Silence

There is a kind of closeness
that doesn't speak.

It just sits.

Love, Revised

Love now feels steadier.

Less fireworks.
More warmth.

It listens.
It adapts.
It grows quieter
without growing smaller.

Watching Time Work

Time doesn't rush.

It reshapes.

What Remains After Passion

After desire fades,
attention remains.

And attention,
given freely,
is its own form
of devotion.

SECTION V — Meaning, Mortality & Legacy

The Question That Arrives Late

It isn't
"What did I achieve?"

It's
"How did I live
while trying?"

Talking to My Future Self

If you're reading this
from a place I cannot imagine yet,
I hope you remember
how uncertain everything once felt.

I hope you don't edit the past
to make it cleaner than it was.

Remember the hesitation.
The doubt that slowed you down.
The nights when progress felt imagined.

Those moments mattered.

They built the patience
you now take for granted.

If life has been kind,
don't confuse comfort
with superiority.

If life has been difficult,
don't confuse struggle
with failure.

I hope you stayed curious.
I hope you learned when to stop pushing
and when to keep going.

Most of all,
I hope you remained honest—
with others,

with yourself,
with the life you chose
instead of the one
you were told to want.

Mortality, Plainly

Death is not dramatic.

It's a closing
without commentary.

The Meaning We Build

Meaning is not discovered.

It's assembled
from choices made
without guarantees.

It lives in consistency.
In showing up
when no one is watching.

It grows quietly—
through effort aligned with values,
through kindness without transaction,
through learning when to let go.

Meaning doesn't announce itself.
It accumulates.

And one day,
you realize
you've been living it
all along.

What I No Longer Fear

I no longer fear
being ordinary.

I fear being absent
from my own life.

Peace, Defined

Peace is not the absence of struggle.

It’s the absence
of unnecessary resistance.

It’s knowing
which battles matter
and which ones
were never yours to fight.

The Long View

Seen from far enough away,
most things soften.

Regret loses its edge.
Urgency quiets.
The need to prove dissolves.

What remains
are patterns—
how you treated people,
how you handled power,
how you responded
when things didn't go your way.

Legacy is not a monument.
It's a residue.

The emotional footprint
you leave behind.

What a Good Life Looks Like

A good life
is not loud.

It is consistent,
considerate,
awake.

Making Peace with Unfinished Things

Some goals remain incomplete.

Some questions stay open.

And that's not failure—
it's realism.

A life fully lived
still leaves margins.

The Last Long Thought

If I could leave one thing behind,
it wouldn't be advice.

It would be permission.

Permission to move at your pace.
To change direction without apology.
To measure success privately.

Permission to rest.
To begin again.
To stop explaining yourself.

Life is not a performance.

It is a practice.

And you are allowed
to practice imperfectly.

Gratitude, Quietly

I'm grateful
not for ease,
but for endurance.

Laurels of Life

The laurels of life
are not given.

They are earned quietly—
through patience,
through repair,
through choosing presence
over perfection.

They are not worn.
They are carried.

In the way you listen.
In the way you stay.
In the way you allow yourself
to keep becoming.

This is not a victory lap.

It is a recognition—
that living fully
was never about winning.

It was about showing up
with care,
with courage,
with enough honesty
to make the journey
worth remembering.

Section VI — Still Becoming

Morning Without Urgency

I wake up
without negotiating with the future.

Nothing is late.
Nothing is owed.

The day opens
like a door
that trusts me.

Enough

I once mistook
more
for better.

Now I recognize
enough
by the way it lets me breathe.

After Apologies

Some apologies arrive late.
Some never arrive at all.

Healing happens anyway
when you stop waiting
for permission.

The Pace I Keep Now

I walk
as if the ground
is not going anywhere.

Because it isn't.

Quiet Confidence

Confidence is no longer loud.

It doesn't explain itself.
It doesn't rush to be seen.

It stays.

What I Don't Carry Anymore

I stopped carrying
other people's expectations
like unpaid debt.

Ordinary Courage

It takes courage
to choose a simple life
in a world
addicted to spectacle.

Unlearning

Unlearning
is harder than learning.

It asks you
to let go
of what once protected you.

The Space Between Tasks

Life doesn't happen
inside achievements.

It happens
between them.

Still Becoming

I am not finished.
I am not broken.

I am
still becoming.

The Version That Survived

There is a version of me
that survived things
no one applauded.

It learned restraint
before optimism.
It learned patience
before clarity.

That version doesn't speak often,
but when it does,
I listen.

Choosing Peace Daily

Peace is not a destination.
It's a daily decision.

It's choosing silence
over winning arguments.
Choosing rest
over proving resilience.

Peace requires discipline—
the discipline to stop escalating
what doesn't deserve intensity.

After the Noise

After the noise fades,
what remains
is not emptiness.

It's discernment.

You learn what deserves attention
and what only borrowed it.

The Work That Matters Now

The work that matters now
doesn't pay in applause.

It pays in alignment.
In waking without dread.
In ending days
without regret.

Letting the Day Be the Day

Not every day
needs a purpose.

Some days
just need permission
to exist
without improvement.

A Softer Strength

Strength used to mean endurance.

Now it means boundaries.
It means stopping early.
It means saying no
without justification.

The Long View of Mistakes

Mistakes shrink
when seen from far enough away.

They become data,
not definitions.

Learning Contentment

Contentment is learned slowly,
through disappointment,
through excess,
through clarity.

It's not settling.
It's selecting.

When Nothing Is Missing

There are moments
when nothing is missing.

They don't last long,
but they teach you
what is possible.

Staying Present

Presence is effortful.
It resists distraction.
It refuses escape.

But it rewards you
with a life
that feels inhabited.

Life After Proving

There is a life
after proving yourself.

After the need to be impressive.
After measuring worth
by recognition.

In that life,
you choose differently.

You stop explaining your choices.
You stop racing invisible competitors.
You stop rehearsing conversations
that never happen.

Time expands.
Not because you have more of it,
but because you waste less of it
on comparison.

You still work.
You still care.
But the urgency has softened.

You finally understand:
meaning was never withheld—
it was waiting
for you to slow down enough
to notice it.

Rebuilding Without Drama

Rebuilding is rarely cinematic.

It looks like quiet mornings,
repeated decisions,
small corrections.

No announcements.
No redemption arcs.

Just consistency
where chaos used to live.

And somehow,
that's enough.

The Life I Actually Live

I no longer live the life
I imagined.

I live the life
I wake up inside.

And it turns out
that presence
is more reliable
than fantasy.

Time, Reconsidered

Time does not rush you.
People do.

Time simply unfolds—
patient, indifferent, honest.

When you stop fighting it,
it teaches you how to live
without panic.

Making Peace With Cycles

Not everything improves forever.

Some things return.
Some lessons repeat.
Some seasons revisit you
with new questions.

Growth is not escape.
It is familiarity
handled better.

The Weight I Choose Now

I still carry weight—
but now I choose which weight
is worth carrying.

That choice
changes everything.

After Ambition

Ambition once moved me forward.

Now discernment does.

I am no longer interested
in becoming more—
only in becoming clearer.

Staying Human

Staying human
is an act of resistance.

Against speed.
Against numbness.
Against abstraction.

It means feeling
without drowning.
Caring
without collapsing.

What Maturity Looks Like

Maturity isn't knowing everything.

It's knowing
what no longer deserves
your energy.

The Ongoing Life

There is no final version.

No completed self.
No permanent arrival.

There is only
the ongoing life—
asking for attention,
honesty,
and care.

And that
is enough.

About the Author

Born on **25 June 1998**,
graduated and mastered in Mathematics.
I learned early
that education begins in classrooms
and matures in experience.

A degree confirmed study in one field,
not the boundaries of curiosity,
nor the reach of understanding
across many.

I write where disciplines meet—
self-help, self-discovery, poetry,
philosophy, and humanity—
with more than **fifty books** written,
and more than **ten that found readers around the world**.

My work listens to the interior life:
to perseverance shaped by struggle,
to faith tested quietly,
to resilience that does not announce itself.

Beyond writing,
I continue toward a wider purpose—
building, learning, giving—
working toward a life that joins
entrepreneurship, philanthropy,
and philosophy.

The work continues.
So do I.

www.ingramcontent.com/pod-product-compliance
Lightning Source LLC
Chambersburg PA
CBHW022157160726
48282CB00024B/229
9789356928084